100 DAYS OF
Self-Discovery

A Guided Journal for Women to
Build Self-Esteem and
Self- Confidence

THIS JOURNAL BELONGS TO:

100 DAYS OF
Self-Discovery

Copyright © Laura Lacy-Thompson, 2024.

All rights reserved. No part of this journal may be reproduced, distributed, or transmitted in any form or by any means, including photocopying, recording, or other electronic or mechanical methods, without the prior written permission of the publisher, except in the case of brief quotations embodied in critical reviews and certain other noncommercial uses permitted by copyright law. For permission requests, write to the publisher at laura@newjourneylifecoaching.com

Contents

Welcome 5
How to Use This Journal.. 6
The Importance of Self-Esteem & Self-Confidence........................ 7
Self-Confidence Assessment.. 8
100 Journal Prompts for Exploring & Elevating
Self-Esteem &Confidence.. 9
Boost Your Self-Esteem Action Checklist................................... 12
Daily and Weekly Journal Pages... 13
25 Affirmations for Self-Esteem & Self-Confidence................... 229

"The journey toward self-discovery is life's greatest adventure"

Arianna Huffington

Welcome 🦋

100 Days of Self-Discovery: A Guided Journal for Women to Build Self-Esteem and Confidence

About This Journal
This journal is designed for women who want to understand themselves better and build strong self-esteem and self-confidence. Over the next 100 days, you will engage with daily prompts, morning and evening check-ins, and weekly reflections.

Why 100 Days?
Committing to 100 days allows you to develop and reinforce new positive beliefs and habits. You have enough time to integrate these practices into your daily routine for lasting change and to wire in new positive thoughts and beliefs that will positively affect how you feel about yourself.

Benefits of This Journal
- **Increased Self-Awareness**: Regular reflection helps you understand yourself better.
- **Enhanced Self-Esteem:** Affirmations and prompts help build your confidence.
- **Greater Self-Confidence**: Honest exploration of your thoughts and feelings leads to self-acceptance and increased confidence.
- **Improved Mental Well-being**: Journaling reduces stress and improves mood.

By using this journal for the next 100 days, you are taking an important step towards becoming more confident and self-assured. Be kind to yourself and let go of perfectionism. Enjoy the process, and celebrate your growth.

Thank you for choosing this journal. I wish you the best on your journey of self-discovery, self-esteem, and self-confidence.

How to Use This Journal

This journal is designed to be easy to use and fit into your daily routine. Here's how you can get the most out of it:

Daily

- **Journal Prompt:** Each day, you'll select a new prompt to guide your reflections. Spend a few minutes writing your thoughts and insights. Choose a prompt that resonates with you on that day.
- **Morning: Check-In**: Start your day with a morning check-in, using the provided affirmations to set a positive tone. Set your intention and the self-belief the action you want to take.
- **Evening check-in**: Reflect on your progress, experiences to release the day, be aware of what went well and clear your mind.

Weekly

- **Choose from the self-esteem and confidence actions to practice each week.**
- **Weekly Reflection:** At the end of each week, take some time to review your entries. Reflect on your self-discovery journey and your feelings over the week. This helps you track your growth and understand your patterns.

Use this journal as a tool to support your journey toward greater self-esteem self-confidence. Enjoy the process and celebrate your growth.

The Importance of Self-Esteem and Confidence

Self-esteem refers to your overall sense of worth and value. It encompasses how you feel about yourself, including your abilities, appearance, and overall identity. High self-esteem means having a positive perception of yourself, while low self-esteem involves a more negative view. Psychological theories suggest that self-esteem is influenced by your personal experiences, social interactions, and internal thought patterns. It plays a crucial role in your mental health, affecting your behavior, relationships, and overall well-being.

Self-confidence is your belief in your abilities to succeed in specific situations or accomplish tasks. It reflects your trust in your skills, judgments, and decisions. Unlike self-esteem, which is more about overall self-worth, self-confidence can vary depending on the context. For example, you might have high self-confidence in your academic abilities but low self-confidence in social situations. This trait is often developed through experience, practice, and positive reinforcement.

While self-esteem and self-confidence are related, they are distinct concepts. **Self-esteem is a broader evaluation of your overall worth, encompassing feelings of self-acceptance and self-respect. In contrast, self-confidence is more specific, relating to your belief in your abilities to perform certain tasks or face particular challenges.** However, the two can influence each other; for instance, consistent success in specific areas can boost your self-confidence, which in turn can enhance your overall self-esteem. Conversely, low self-esteem can undermine self-confidence, making you doubt your capabilities even in areas where you have skills. Thus, nurturing both is important for your personal growth and psychological well-being.

Over the next 100 days this journal will guide you to enhancing both so you create the most fulfilling life and tap into your full potential.

Self-Confidence Assessment

Instructions: For each statement below, rate how strongly you agree or disagree using the following scale: 1 = Strongly Disagree. 2 = Disagree. 3 = Neutral 4 = Agree   5 = Strongly Agree

	1	2	3	4	5
I believe in my ability to overcome challenges.		✓			
I am confident in my skills and talents.		✓			
I trust my judgment in making important decisions.	✓				
I am capable of achieving my goals.				✓	
I feel confident speaking in front of others.	✓				
I handle setbacks well and bounce back quickly.	✓				
I am comfortable taking on new responsibilities.	✓				
I feel proud of my accomplishments.					✓
I am persistent and do not give up easily.				✓	
I am good at finding solutions to problems.	✓				
I maintain a positive attitude even in difficult situations.	✓				
I believe I deserve success and happiness.				✓	
I am confident in my ability to learn new things.				✓	
I feel comfortable expressing my opinions and ideas.		✓			
	6	8	12		5

15-30: Low self-confidence: This range indicates a need to work on building your confidence. You may benefit from positive affirmations, self-improvement exercises, and possibly seeking support from a mentor or therapist.

31-45: Moderate self-confidence: You have a balanced view of your abilities but may still doubt yourself at times. Focus on reinforcing your strengths and addressing any specific areas where you lack self-belief.

46-60: High self-confidence: You generally feel confident in your abilities and handle challenges well.

61-75: Very high self-confidence: You have a strong sense of self-confidence and believe firmly in your abilities.

100 Journal Prompts for Exploring and Elevating Self-Esteem and Self-Confidence

1. What are three qualities you admire about yourself and why?
2. Describe a recent achievement and how it made you feel.
3. Write about a time when you felt proud of yourself. What happened?
4. What are three things you're grateful for today?
5. How do you define self-acceptance?
6. List five things you love about your personality.
7. How do you show yourself compassion on tough days?
8. Describe a moment when you overcame a significant challenge.
9. What positive impact have you had on someone else's life?
10. Write a letter to your younger self with advice and encouragement.
11. What does self-belief mean to you?
12. How do you handle self-doubt?
13. Write about a fear you've overcome and how it changed you.
14. What are three goals you're currently working towards and why?
15. How do you celebrate your successes, big or small?
16. Describe a person you admire and the qualities they possess.
17. How do you practice self-care?
18. What are your strengths? How do they help you in daily life?
19. Write about a mistake you made and what you learned from it.
20. How do you stay motivated when working towards a goal?
21. What limiting beliefs are holding you back?
22. Write about a time when you surprised yourself with your capabilities.
23. How do you maintain a positive mindset?
24. Describe a compliment you received recently and how it made you feel.
25. What are three things you appreciate about your body?
26. How do you handle criticism?
27. Write about a hobby or activity that brings you joy.
28. What is your personal definition of success?
29. How do you nurture your mental and emotional well-being?
30. Write a letter to yourself filled with love and acceptance.
31. What does self-love look like for you?
32. How do you maintain healthy boundaries in relationships?
33. What are your core values and how do they guide your life?

100 Journal Prompts for Exploring and Elevating Self-Esteem and Self-Confidence

34. Write about a dream you have and the steps you're taking to achieve it.
35. How do you stay true to yourself in challenging situations?
36. Describe a moment when you felt completely at peace with yourself.
37. What are three affirmations you can use to boost your self-belief?
38. How do you cope with failure or setbacks?
39. Write about a time when you felt incredibly confident.
40. What are three things you've accomplished this year that you're proud of?
41. How do you balance self-improvement with self-acceptance?
42. Describe a time when you trusted your intuition and it paid off.
43. What makes you unique and special?
44. How do you practice gratitude in your daily life?
45. Write about a person who has positively influenced your self-belief.
46. How do you stay grounded in your values and beliefs?
47. What is your biggest source of inspiration?
48. How do you manage stress and anxiety?
49. Describe a time when you took a risk and what you learned from it.
50. What are three qualities you admire in others that you also see in yourself?
51. How do you cultivate a growth mindset?
52. Write about a recent challenge and how you overcame it.
53. What is your personal mantra and why?
54. How do you ensure you're living authentically?
55. Describe a moment when you felt empowered.
56. What are three habits that support your self-belief?
57. How do you deal with negative self-talk?
58. Write about a time when you felt truly happy and content.
59. What are your passions and how do they contribute to your sense of self?
60. How do you maintain a balance between work and personal life?
61. Describe a time when you made a positive change in your life.
62. What are three things you do to boost your mood?
63. How do you stay focused on your goals?
64. Write about a person who believes in you and why their support is meaningful.
65. How do you practice mindfulness and stay present?
66. What are your strengths and how do they help you navigate life?
67. How do you handle comparison to others?

100 Journal Prompts for Exploring and Elevating Self-Esteem and Self-Confidence

68. Write about a time when you felt unstoppable. 69. What are three ways you can show yourself more compassion? 70. How do you celebrate your individuality?
71. Describe a time when you felt a strong sense of purpose.
72. What are your greatest accomplishments and what do they mean to you?
73. How do you build and maintain healthy relationships?
74. Write about a time when you helped someone and how it impacted you.
75. How do you stay motivated during difficult times?
76. What are three things you do to take care of your mental health?
77. How do you ensure you're living a fulfilling life?
78. Describe a moment when you felt deeply connected to yourself.
79. What are three things you've learned about yourself this year?
80. How do you practice self-forgiveness?
81. Write about a goal you achieved and the journey to get there.
82. What are your core beliefs and how do they shape your life?
83. How do you stay positive and hopeful?
84. Describe a time when you felt immense gratitude.
85. What are three ways you can improve your self-belief?
86. How do you nurture your creativity?
87. Write about a time when you felt a sense of belonging.
88. How do you maintain a healthy self-image?
89. What are your long-term goals and how do you plan to achieve them?
90. How do you stay resilient in the face of adversity?
91. Describe a moment when you felt truly alive.
92. What are three things you've done this month that you're proud of?
93. How do you maintain a sense of balance and harmony in your life?
94. Write about a person who inspires you and why.
95. How do you cultivate inner peace?
96. What are three things you love about your life?
97. How do you handle and learn from failure?
98. Describe a time when you felt at your best.
99. What are your daily rituals for self-care?
100. How do you stay committed to your personal growth?

Boost Your Self-Esteem Action Checklist

Choose 1 action weekly to focus on from this list to enhance your confidence and self-esteem.

- ✓ Celebrate small wins daily.
- ✓ Do things that make you happy.
- ✓ Stop comparing yourself to others
- ✓ Embrace your imperfections.
- ✓ Focus on what you can change.
- ✓ Let go of what you can't control.
- ✓ Surround yourself with positive people
- ✓ Learn a new skill
- ✓ Do something that makes you uncomfortable.
- ✓ Get creative. Being creative puts you in flow.
- ✓ Change your self-talk. Speak kindly to yourself.
- ✓ Update your style/appearance. Look your best daily.
- ✓ Create and maintain strong personal boundaries
- ✓ Learn something new.
- ✓ Approach challenges with a beginner's mindset.
- ✓ Sit up straight and walk tall.
- ✓ Engage in the basics of self-care; exercise, sleep & healthy eating.
- ✓ Be kind to others.
- ✓ Create a list of things you like about yourself.

Weekly Reflection

What went well this week?

_____
_____
_____
_____
_____
_____
_____

What changes have you noticed when it comes to your self-esteem and self-confidence?

_____
_____
_____
_____
_____
_____
_____
_____

What resistance, if any, have you felt to this process? How might you shift this?

_____
_____
_____
_____
_____
_____

Self-Esteem Scale

Self-Esteem /confidence action for the coming week?

Good Morning

Date: _____

Daily Intention
What do you want this day to be about?

_____
_____
_____

Today's Affirmation

_____

Actions	Self-Care
_____	_____
_____	_____
_____	_____
_____	_____

Good Evening

Today's Accomplishment
What went well today?

_____
_____

Today's Challenge
What didn't go well today?

_____
_____

Brain Dump

_____
_____
_____

Journal Prompt

Choose one of the prompts that resonates with you and write/draw/doodle what comes up for you.

Good Morning

Date: _____

Daily Intention — What do you want this day to be about?

_____
_____
_____

Today's Affirmation

_____

Actions	Self-Care
_____	_____
_____	_____
_____	_____
_____	_____

Good Evening

Today's Accomplishment — What went well today?

_____
_____

Today's Challenge — What didn't go well today?

_____
_____

Brain Dump

_____
_____
_____

Journal Prompt

Choose one of the prompts that resonates with you and write/draw/doodle what comes up for you.

Good Morning

Date: _____

Daily Intention What do you want this day to be about?

_____
_____
_____

Today's Affirmation

_____

Actions	Self-Care
_____	_____
_____	_____
_____	_____
_____	_____

Good Evening

Today's Accomplishment What went well today?

_____
_____

Today's Challenge What didn't go well today?

_____
_____

Brain Dump

_____
_____
_____

Journal Prompt

Choose one of the prompts that resonates with you and write/draw/doodle what comes up for you.

Good Morning

Date: _____

Daily Intention — What do you want this day to be about?
_____
_____
_____

Today's Affirmation

Actions | Self-Care
_____ | _____
_____ | _____
_____ | _____
_____ | _____

Good Evening

Today's Accomplishment | What went well today?
_____
_____

Today's Challenge | What didn't go well today?
_____
_____

Brain Dump
_____
_____
_____

Journal Prompt

Choose one of the prompts that resonates with you and write/draw/doodle what comes up for you.

Good Morning

Date: _____

Daily Intention — What do you want this day to be about?

_____
_____
_____

Today's Affirmation

Actions

_____
_____
_____
_____

Self-Care

_____
_____
_____
_____

Good Evening

Today's Accomplishment — What went well today?

_____
_____

Today's Challenge — What didn't go well today?

_____
_____

Brain Dump

_____
_____
_____

Journal Prompt

Choose one of the prompts that resonates with you and write/draw/doodle what comes up for you.

Good Morning

Date: _____

Daily Intention What do you want this day to be about?

_____
_____
_____

Today's Affirmation

Actions | **Self-Care**

_____ _____
_____ _____
_____ _____
_____ _____

Good Evening

Today's Accomplishment What went well today?

_____
_____

Today's Challenge What didn't go well today?

_____
_____

Brain Dump

_____
_____
_____

Journal Prompt

Choose one of the prompts that resonates with you and write/draw/doodle what comes up for you.

Good Morning

Date: _____

Daily Intention What do you want this day to be about?

_____
_____
_____

Today's Affirmation

_____

Actions	Self-Care
_____	_____
_____	_____
_____	_____
_____	_____

Good Evening

Today's Accomplishment What went well today?

_____
_____

Today's Challenge What didn't go well today?

_____
_____

Brain Dump

_____
_____
_____

Journal Prompt

Choose one of the prompts that resonates with you and write/draw/doodle what comes up for you.

Weekly Reflection

What went well this week?

_____
_____
_____
_____
_____
_____

What changes have you noticed when it comes to your self-esteem and self- confidence?

_____
_____
_____
_____
_____
_____

What resistance, if any, have you felt to this process? How might you shift this?

_____
_____
_____
_____
_____

Self-Esteem Scale

Self-Esteem /confidence action for the coming week?

Good Morning 🦋

Date: _____

Daily Intention — What do you want this day to be about?

_____
_____
_____

Today's Affirmation

_____

Actions	Self-Care
_____	_____
_____	_____
_____	_____
_____	_____

Good Evening 🦋

Today's Accomplishment — What went well today?

_____
_____

Today's Challenge — What didn't go well today?

_____
_____

Brain Dump

_____
_____
_____

Journal Prompt

Choose one of the prompts that resonates with you and write/draw/doodle what comes up for you.

Good Morning

Date: _____

Daily Intention — What do you want this day to be about?

_____
_____
_____

Today's Affirmation

Actions

_____
_____
_____
_____

Self-Care

_____
_____
_____

Good Evening

Today's Accomplishment — What went well today?

_____
_____

Today's Challenge — What didn't go well today?

_____
_____

Brain Dump

_____
_____
_____

Journal Prompt

Choose one of the prompts that resonates with you and write/draw/doodle what comes up for you.

Good Morning

Date: _____

Daily Intention What do you want this day to be about?

_____
_____
_____

Today's Affirmation

_____

Actions   **Self-Care**

_____   _____
_____   _____
_____   _____
_____   _____

Good Evening

Today's Accomplishment   What went well today?

_____
_____

Today's Challenge   What didn't go well today?

_____
_____

Brain Dump

_____
_____
_____

Journal Prompt

Choose one of the prompts that resonates with you and write/draw/doodle what comes up for you.

Good Morning

Date: _____

Daily Intention — What do you want this day to be about?

_____
_____
_____

Today's Affirmation

_____

Actions	Self-Care
_____	_____
_____	_____
_____	_____
_____	_____

Good Evening

Today's Accomplishment — What went well today?

_____
_____

Today's Challenge — What didn't go well today?

_____
_____

Brain Dump

_____
_____
_____

Good Morning

Date: _____

Daily Intention — What do you want this day to be about?
_____
_____
_____

Today's Affirmation

_____
_____
_____

Actions   **Self-Care**
_____   _____
_____   _____
_____   _____

Good Evening

Today's Accomplishment   **What went well today?**
_____
_____

Today's Challenge   **What didn't go well today?**
_____
_____

Brain Dump
_____
_____
_____

Journal Prompt

Choose one of the prompts that resonates with you and write/draw/doodle what comes up for you.

Good Morning

Date: _____

Daily Intention — What do you want this day to be about?

_____
_____
_____

Today's Affirmation

_____

Actions	Self-Care
_____	_____
_____	_____
_____	_____
_____	_____

Good Evening

Today's Accomplishment — What went well today?

_____
_____

Today's Challenge — What didn't go well today?

_____
_____

Brain Dump

_____
_____
_____

Journal Prompt

Choose one of the prompts that resonates with you and write/draw/doodle what comes up for you.

Good Morning

Date: _____

Daily Intention
What do you want this day to be about?

_____
_____
_____

Today's Affirmation

Actions
_____
_____
_____
_____

Self-Care
_____
_____
_____
_____

Good Evening

Today's Accomplishment
What went well today?
_____
_____

Today's Challenge
What didn't go well today?
_____
_____

Brain Dump
_____
_____
_____

Journal Prompt

Choose one of the prompts that resonates with you and write/draw/doodle what comes up for you.

Weekly Reflection

What went well this week?
_____
_____
_____
_____
_____
_____
_____

What changes have you noticed when it comes to your self-esteem and self- confidence?
_____
_____
_____
_____
_____
_____
_____

What resistance, if any, have you felt to this process? How might you shift this?
_____
_____
_____
_____
_____
_____

Self-Esteem Scale

Self-Esteem /confidence action for the coming week?

43

Good Morning

Date: _____

Daily Intention · What do you want this day to be about?

_____
_____
_____

Today's Affirmation

Actions · Self-Care

_____ · _____
_____ · _____
_____ · _____
_____ · _____

Good Evening

Today's Accomplishment · What went well today?

_____
_____

Today's Challenge · What didn't go well today?

_____
_____

Brain Dump

_____
_____
_____

Journal Prompt

Choose one of the prompts that resonates with you and write/draw/doodle what comes up for you.

Good Morning

Date: _____

Daily Intention — What do you want this day to be about?

_____
_____
_____

Today's Affirmation

Actions   **Self-Care**

_____   _____
_____   _____
_____   _____
_____   _____

Good Evening

Today's Accomplishment   **What went well today?**

_____
_____

Today's Challenge   **What didn't go well today?**

_____
_____

Brain Dump

_____
_____
_____

Journal Prompt

Choose one of the prompts that resonates with you and write/draw/doodle what comes up for you.

Good Morning

Date: _____

Daily Intention
What do you want this day to be about?

_____
_____
_____

Today's Affirmation

Actions
_____
_____
_____
_____

Self-Care
_____
_____
_____
_____

Good Evening

Today's Accomplishment
What went well today?
_____
_____

Today's Challenge
What didn't go well today?
_____
_____

Brain Dump
_____
_____
_____

Journal Prompt

Choose one of the prompts that resonates with you and write/draw/doodle what comes up for you.

Good Morning

Date: _____

Daily Intention — What do you want this day to be about?

_____
_____
_____

Today's Affirmation

_____

Actions	Self-Care
_____	_____
_____	_____
_____	_____
_____	_____

Good Evening

Today's Accomplishment — What went well today?

_____
_____

Today's Challenge — What didn't go well today?

_____
_____

Brain Dump

_____
_____
_____

Journal Prompt

Choose one of the prompts that resonates with you and write/draw/doodle what comes up for you.

Good Morning

Date: _____

Daily Intention
What do you want this day to be about?

_____
_____
_____

Today's Affirmation

_____
_____
_____

Actions
- _____
- _____
- _____
- _____

Self-Care
- _____
- _____
- _____
- _____

Good Evening

Today's Accomplishment
What went well today?

_____
_____

Today's Challenge
What didn't go well today?

_____
_____

Brain Dump

_____
_____
_____

Journal Prompt

Choose one of the prompts that resonates with you and write/draw/doodle what comes up for you.

Good Morning

Date: _____

Daily Intention What do you want this day to be about?

_____
_____
_____

Today's Affirmation

Actions **Self-Care**

_____ _____
_____ _____
_____ _____
_____ _____

Good Evening

Today's Accomplishment What went well today?

_____
_____

Today's Challenge What didn't go well today?

_____
_____

Brain Dump

_____
_____
_____

Journal Prompt

Choose one of the prompts that resonates with you and write/draw/doodle what comes up for you.

Good Morning

Date: _____

Daily Intention — What do you want this day to be about?

_____
_____
_____

Today's Affirmation

_____
_____
_____

Actions	Self-Care
_____	_____
_____	_____
_____	_____
_____	_____

Good Evening

Today's Accomplishment — What went well today?

_____
_____

Today's Challenge — What didn't go well today?

_____
_____

Brain Dump

_____
_____
_____

Journal Prompt

Choose one of the prompts that resonates with you and write/draw/doodle what comes up for you.

Weekly Reflection

What went well this week?

_____
_____
_____
_____
_____
_____
_____

What changes have you noticed when it comes to your self-esteem and self-confidence?

_____
_____
_____
_____
_____
_____
_____

What resistance, if any, have you felt to this process? How might you shift this?

_____
_____
_____
_____
_____
_____

Self-Esteem Scale	Self-Esteem /confidence action for the coming week?

Good Morning

Date: _____

Daily Intention — What do you want this day to be about?

_____
_____
_____

Today's Affirmation

_____

Actions	Self-Care
_____	_____
_____	_____
_____	_____
_____	_____

Good Evening

Today's Accomplishment — What went well today?

_____
_____

Today's Challenge — What didn't go well today?

_____
_____

Brain Dump

_____
_____
_____

Journal Prompt

Choose one of the prompts that resonates with you and write/draw/doodle what comes up for you.

Good Morning

Date: _____

Daily Intention — What do you want this day to be about?

_____
_____
_____

Today's Affirmation

Actions	Self-Care
_____	_____
_____	_____
_____	_____
_____	_____

Good Evening

Today's Accomplishment — What went well today?

_____
_____

Today's Challenge — What didn't go well today?

_____
_____

Brain Dump

_____
_____
_____

Journal Prompt

Choose one of the prompts that resonates with you and write/draw/doodle what comes up for you.

Good Morning

Date: _____

Daily Intention — What do you want this day to be about?

_____
_____
_____

Today's Affirmation

_____

Actions	Self-Care
_____	_____
_____	_____
_____	_____
_____	_____

Good Evening

Today's Accomplishment — What went well today?

_____
_____

Today's Challenge — What didn't go well today?

_____
_____

Brain Dump

_____
_____
_____

Journal Prompt

Choose one of the prompts that resonates with you and write/draw/doodle what comes up for you.

Good Morning

Date: _____

Daily Intention What do you want this day to be about?

_____
_____
_____

Today's Affirmation

Actions

_____
_____
_____
_____

Self-Care

_____
_____
_____
_____

Good Evening

Today's Accomplishment What went well today?

_____
_____

Today's Challenge What didn't go well today?

_____
_____

Brain Dump

_____
_____
_____

Journal Prompt

Choose one of the prompts that resonates with you and write/draw/doodle what comes up for you.

66

Good Morning

Date: _____

Daily Intention What do you want this day to be about?

_____
_____
_____

Today's Affirmation

Actions | **Self-Care**

_____ _____
_____ _____
_____ _____

Good Evening

Today's Accomplishment What went well today?
_____
_____

Today's Challenge What didn't go well today?
_____
_____

Brain Dump
_____
_____
_____

Journal Prompt

Choose one of the prompts that resonates with you and write/draw/doodle what comes up for you.

Good Morning

Date: _____

Daily Intention — What do you want this day to be about?

_____
_____
_____

Today's Affirmation

_____
_____
_____

Actions	Self-Care
_____	_____
_____	_____
_____	_____

Good Evening

Today's Accomplishment — What went well today?

_____
_____

Today's Challenge — What didn't go well today?

_____
_____

Brain Dump

_____
_____

Journal Prompt

Choose one of the prompts that resonates with you and write/draw/doodle what comes up for you.

Good Morning

Date: _____

Daily Intention — What do you want this day to be about?

_____
_____
_____

Today's Affirmation

_____

Actions	Self-Care
_____	_____
_____	_____
_____	_____
_____	_____

Good Evening

Today's Accomplishment — What went well today?

_____
_____

Today's Challenge — What didn't go well today?

_____
_____

Brain Dump

_____
_____
_____

Journal Prompt

Choose one of the prompts that resonates with you and write/draw/doodle what comes up for you.

Weekly Reflection

What went well this week?

_____
_____
_____
_____
_____
_____

What changes have you noticed when it comes to your self-esteem and self- confidence?

_____
_____
_____
_____
_____
_____

What resistance, if any, have you felt to this process? How might you shift this?

_____
_____
_____
_____
_____
_____

Self-Esteem Scale

Self-Esteem /confidence action for the coming week?

Good Morning

Date: _____

Daily Intention   What do you want this day to be about?

_____
_____
_____

Today's Affirmation

Actions   Self-Care

_____   _____
_____   _____
_____   _____
_____   _____

Good Evening

Today's Accomplishment   What went well today?

_____
_____

Today's Challenge   What didn't go well today?

_____
_____

Brain Dump

_____
_____
_____

Journal Prompt

Choose one of the prompts that resonates with you and write/draw/doodle what comes up for you.

Good Morning

Date: _____

Daily Intention   What do you want this day to be about?
_____
_____
_____

Today's Affirmation

_____
_____

Actions   Self-Care
_____   _____
_____   _____
_____   _____
_____   _____

Good Evening

Today's Accomplishment   What went well today?
_____
_____

Today's Challenge   What didn't go well today?
_____
_____

Brain Dump
_____
_____
_____

Journal Prompt

Choose one of the prompts that resonates with you and write/draw/doodle what comes up for you.

Good Morning

Date: _____

Daily Intention — What do you want this day to be about?

_____
_____
_____

Today's Affirmation

_____

Actions	Self-Care
_____	_____
_____	_____
_____	_____
_____	_____

Good Evening

Today's Accomplishment — What went well today?

_____
_____

Today's Challenge — What didn't go well today?

_____
_____

Brain Dump

_____
_____
_____

Journal Prompt

Choose one of the prompts that resonates with you and write/draw/doodle what comes up for you.

Good Morning 🦋

Date: _____

Daily Intention — What do you want this day to be about?

_____
_____
_____

Today's Affirmation

_____
_____
_____
_____

Actions	Self-Care
_____	_____
_____	_____
_____	_____
_____	_____

Good Evening 🦋

Today's Accomplishment — What went well today?

_____
_____

Today's Challenge — What didn't go well today?

_____
_____

Brain Dump

_____
_____
_____

Journal Prompt

Choose one of the prompts that resonates with you and write/draw/doodle what comes up for you.

Good Morning

Date: _____

Daily Intention — What do you want this day to be about?

_____
_____
_____

Today's Affirmation

Actions   **Self-Care**

_____   _____
_____   _____
_____   _____
_____   _____

Good Evening

Today's Accomplishment   **What went well today?**

_____
_____

Today's Challenge   **What didn't go well today?**

_____
_____

Brain Dump

_____
_____
_____

Journal Prompt

Choose one of the prompts that resonates with you and write/draw/doodle what comes up for you.

83

Good Morning

Date: _____

Daily Intention — What do you want this day to be about?

_____
_____
_____

Today's Affirmation

_____

Actions	Self-Care
_____	_____
_____	_____
_____	_____
_____	_____

Good Evening

Today's Accomplishment — What went well today?

_____
_____

Today's Challenge — What didn't go well today?

_____
_____

Brain Dump

_____
_____
_____

Journal Prompt

Choose one of the prompts that resonates with you and write/draw/doodle what comes up for you.

Good Morning

Date: _____

Daily Intention   What do you want this day to be about?

_____
_____
_____

Today's Affirmation

Actions   Self-Care

_____   _____
_____   _____
_____   _____
_____   _____

Good Evening

Today's Accomplishment   What went well today?

_____
_____

Today's Challenge   What didn't go well today?

_____
_____

Brain Dump

_____
_____
_____

Journal Prompt

Choose one of the prompts that resonates with you and write/draw/doodle what comes up for you.

Weekly Reflection

What went well this week?

_____
_____
_____
_____
_____
_____
_____

What changes have you noticed when it comes to your self-esteem and self-confidence?

_____
_____
_____
_____
_____
_____
_____

What resistance, if any, have you felt to this process? How might you shift this?

_____
_____
_____
_____
_____
_____

Self-Esteem Scale

Self-Esteem /confidence action for the coming week?

Good Morning

Date: _____

Daily Intention   What do you want this day to be about?

_____
_____
_____

Today's Affirmation

_____

Actions	Self-Care
_____	_____
_____	_____
_____	_____
_____	_____

Good Evening

Today's Accomplishment   What went well today?

_____
_____

Today's Challenge   What didn't go well today?

_____
_____

Brain Dump

_____
_____
_____

Journal Prompt

Choose one of the prompts that resonates with you and write/draw/doodle what comes up for you.

Good Morning

Date: _____

Daily Intention — What do you want this day to be about?

_____
_____
_____

Today's Affirmation

Actions

_____
_____
_____
_____

Self-Care

_____
_____
_____
_____

Good Evening

Today's Accomplishment — What went well today?

_____
_____

Today's Challenge — What didn't go well today?

_____
_____

Brain Dump

_____
_____

Journal Prompt

Choose one of the prompts that resonates with you and write/draw/doodle what comes up for you.

Good Morning

Date: _____

Daily Intention
What do you want this day to be about?

_____
_____
_____

Today's Affirmation

_____

Actions
_____
_____
_____
_____

Self-Care
_____
_____
_____
_____

Good Evening

Today's Accomplishment
What went well today?

_____
_____

Today's Challenge
What didn't go well today?

_____
_____

Brain Dump
_____
_____
_____

Journal Prompt

Choose one of the prompts that resonates with you and write/draw/doodle what comes up for you.

Good Morning

Date: _____

Daily Intention — What do you want this day to be about?

_____
_____
_____

Today's Affirmation

Actions	Self-Care
_____	_____
_____	_____
_____	_____
_____	_____

Good Evening

Today's Accomplishment — What went well today?
_____
_____

Today's Challenge — What didn't go well today?
_____
_____

Brain Dump
_____
_____
_____

Journal Prompt

Choose one of the prompts that resonates with you and write/draw/doodle what comes up for you.

Good Morning

Date: _____

Daily Intention — What do you want this day to be about?
_____
_____
_____

Today's Affirmation

Actions	Self-Care
_____	_____
_____	_____
_____	_____

Good Evening

Today's Accomplishment — What went well today?
_____
_____

Today's Challenge — What didn't go well today?
_____
_____

Brain Dump
_____
_____
_____

Journal Prompt

Choose one of the prompts that resonates with you and write/draw/doodle what comes up for you.

Good Morning

Date: _____

Daily Intention — What do you want this day to be about?

_____
_____
_____

Today's Affirmation

_____

Actions	Self-Care
_____	_____
_____	_____
_____	_____
_____	_____

Good Evening

Today's Accomplishment — What went well today?
_____
_____

Today's Challenge — What didn't go well today?
_____
_____

Brain Dump
_____
_____
_____

Journal Prompt

Choose one of the prompts that resonates with you and write/draw/doodle what comes up for you.

Good Morning

Date: _____

Daily Intention — What do you want this day to be about?

_____
_____
_____

Today's Affirmation

[   ]

Actions   **Self-Care**

_____   _____
_____   _____
_____   _____
_____   _____

Good Evening

Today's Accomplishment   What went well today?

_____
_____

Today's Challenge   What didn't go well today?

_____
_____

Brain Dump

_____
_____
_____

Journal Prompt

Choose one of the prompts that resonates with you and write/draw/doodle what comes up for you.

Weekly Reflection

What went well this week?
_____
_____
_____
_____
_____
_____
_____

What changes have you noticed when it comes to your self-esteem and self- confidence?
_____
_____
_____
_____
_____
_____
_____
_____

What resistance, if any, have you felt to this process? How might you shift this?
_____
_____
_____
_____
_____
_____

Self-Esteem Scale

Self-Esteem /confidence action for the coming week?

Good Morning 🦋

Date: _____

Daily Intention   What do you want this day to be about?

_____
_____
_____

Today's Affirmation

Actions   Self-Care

_____   _____
_____   _____
_____   _____
_____   _____

Good Evening 🦋

Today's Accomplishment   What went well today?

_____
_____

Today's Challenge   What didn't go well today?

_____
_____

Brain Dump

_____
_____
_____

Journal Prompt

Choose one of the prompts that resonates with you and write/draw/doodle what comes up for you.

Good Morning

Date: _____

Daily Intention — What do you want this day to be about?

_____
_____
_____

Today's Affirmation

_____
_____
_____
_____

Actions	Self-Care
_____	_____
_____	_____
_____	_____
_____	_____

Good Evening

Today's Accomplishment — What went well today?

_____
_____

Today's Challenge — What didn't go well today?

_____
_____

Brain Dump

_____
_____
_____

Journal Prompt

Choose one of the prompts that resonates with you and write/draw/doodle what comes up for you.

Good Morning

Date: _____

Daily Intention   What do you want this day to be about?

_____
_____
_____

Today's Affirmation

_____
_____
_____
_____

Actions   **Self-Care**

_____   _____
_____   _____
_____   _____
_____   _____

Good Evening

Today's Accomplishment   What went well today?

_____
_____

Today's Challenge   What didn't go well today?

_____
_____

Brain Dump

_____
_____
_____

Journal Prompt

Choose one of the prompts that resonates with you and write/draw/doodle what comes up for you.

Date: _____

Good Morning

Daily Intention — What do you want this day to be about?

_____
_____
_____

Today's Affirmation

Actions

_____
_____
_____
_____

Self-Care

_____
_____
_____
_____

Good Evening

Today's Accomplishment — What went well today?

_____
_____

Today's Challenge — What didn't go well today?

_____
_____

Brain Dump

_____
_____
_____

Journal Prompt

Choose one of the prompts that resonates with you and write/draw/doodle what comes up for you.

Good Morning

Date: _____

Daily Intention
What do you want this day to be about?

_____
_____
_____

Today's Affirmation

_____
_____
_____
_____

Actions	Self-Care
_____	_____
_____	_____
_____	_____
_____	_____

Good Evening

Today's Accomplishment — What went well today?
_____
_____

Today's Challenge — What didn't go well today?
_____
_____

Brain Dump
_____
_____
_____

Journal Prompt

Choose one of the prompts that resonates with you and write/draw/doodle what comes up for you.

Good Morning

Date: _____

Daily Intention — What do you want this day to be about?

_____
_____
_____

Today's Affirmation

_____

Actions	Self-Care
_____	_____
_____	_____
_____	_____
_____	_____

Good Evening

Today's Accomplishment — What went well today?
_____
_____

Today's Challenge — What didn't go well today?
_____
_____

Brain Dump
_____
_____
_____

Journal Prompt

Choose one of the prompts that resonates with you and write/draw/doodle what comes up for you.

115

Good Morning

Date: _____

Daily Intention — What do you want this day to be about?
_____
_____
_____

Today's Affirmation

Actions   Self-Care
_____   _____
_____   _____
_____   _____
_____   _____

Good Evening

Today's Accomplishment   What went well today?
_____
_____

Today's Challenge   What didn't go well today?
_____
_____

Brain Dump
_____
_____
_____

Journal Prompt

Choose one of the prompts that resonates with you and write/draw/doodle what comes up for you.

Weekly Reflection

What went well this week?

_____
_____
_____
_____
_____
_____
_____

What changes have you noticed when it comes to your self-esteem and self-confidence?

_____
_____
_____
_____
_____
_____
_____

What resistance, if any, have you felt to this process? How might you shift this?

_____
_____
_____
_____
_____
_____

Self-Esteem Scale

Self-Esteem /confidence action for the coming week?

Good Morning

Date: _____

Daily Intention 　　　　　　　　What do you want this day to be about?

_____
_____
_____

Today's Affirmation

Actions　　　　　　　　　　　　　　**Self-Care**

_____　　_____
_____　　_____
_____　　_____
_____　　_____

Good Evening

Today's Accomplishment　　　　　　　What went well today?

_____
_____

Today's Challenge　　　　　　　　What didn't go well today?

_____
_____

Brain Dump

_____
_____
_____

Journal Prompt

Choose one of the prompts that resonates with you and write/draw/doodle what comes up for you.

Good Morning

Date: _____

Daily Intention — What do you want this day to be about?
_____
_____
_____

Today's Affirmation

_____

Actions	Self-Care
_____	_____
_____	_____
_____	_____

Good Evening

Today's Accomplishment — What went well today?
_____
_____

Today's Challenge — What didn't go well today?
_____
_____

Brain Dump
_____
_____
_____

Journal Prompt

Choose one of the prompts that resonates with you and write/draw/doodle what comes up for you.

Good Morning

Date: _____

Daily Intention — What do you want this day to be about?

_____
_____
_____

Today's Affirmation

_____

Actions	Self-Care
_____	_____
_____	_____
_____	_____
_____	_____

Good Evening

Today's Accomplishment — What went well today?

_____
_____

Today's Challenge — What didn't go well today?

_____
_____

Brain Dump

_____
_____
_____

Journal Prompt

Choose one of the prompts that resonates with you and write/draw/doodle what comes up for you.

Good Morning

Date: _____

Daily Intention What do you want this day to be about?

_____
_____
_____

Today's Affirmation

Actions | **Self-Care**

_____ | _____
_____ | _____
_____ | _____
_____ | _____

Good Evening

Today's Accomplishment What went well today?

_____
_____

Today's Challenge What didn't go well today?

_____
_____

Brain Dump

_____
_____
_____

Journal Prompt

Choose one of the prompts that resonates with you and write/draw/doodle what comes up for you.

Good Morning

Date: _____

Daily Intention — What do you want this day to be about?

_____
_____
_____

Today's Affirmation

_____
_____
_____

Actions	Self-Care
_____	_____
_____	_____
_____	_____
_____	_____

Good Evening

Today's Accomplishment — What went well today?

_____
_____

Today's Challenge — What didn't go well today?

_____
_____

Brain Dump

_____
_____
_____

Journal Prompt

Choose one of the prompts that resonates with you and write/draw/doodle what comes up for you.

Good Morning

Date: _____

Daily Intention What do you want this day to be about?

_____
_____
_____

Today's Affirmation

_____

Actions **Self-Care**

_____ _____
_____ _____
_____ _____
_____ _____

Good Evening

Today's Accomplishment What went well today?

_____
_____

Today's Challenge What didn't go well today?

_____
_____

Brain Dump

_____
_____
_____

Journal Prompt

Choose one of the prompts that resonates with you and write/draw/doodle what comes up for you.

Good Morning

Date: _____

Daily Intention — What do you want this day to be about?

_____
_____
_____

Today's Affirmation

Actions

_____
_____
_____
_____

Self-Care

_____
_____
_____
_____

Good Evening

Today's Accomplishment — What went well today?

_____
_____

Today's Challenge — What didn't go well today?

_____
_____

Brain Dump

_____
_____
_____

Journal Prompt

Choose one of the prompts that resonates with you and write/draw/doodle what comes up for you.

Weekly Reflection

What went well this week?

_____
_____
_____
_____
_____
_____
_____

What changes have you noticed when it comes to your self-esteem and self- confidence?

_____
_____
_____
_____
_____
_____
_____

What resistance, if any, have you felt to this process? How might you shift this?

_____
_____
_____
_____
_____
_____

Self-Esteem Scale	Self-Esteem /confidence action for the coming week?

Good Morning

Date: _____

Daily Intention What do you want this day to be about?

_____
_____
_____

Today's Affirmation

Actions **Self-Care**

_____ _____
_____ _____
_____ _____
_____ _____

Good Evening

Today's Accomplishment What went well today?

_____
_____

Today's Challenge What didn't go well today?

_____
_____

Brain Dump

_____
_____
_____

Journal Prompt

Choose one of the prompts that resonates with you and write/draw/doodle what comes up for you.

Good Morning

Date: _____

Daily Intention — What do you want this day to be about?
_____
_____
_____

Today's Affirmation

_____
_____
_____

Actions   **Self-Care**
_____   _____
_____   _____
_____   _____
_____   _____

Good Evening

Today's Accomplishment   **What went well today?**
_____
_____

Today's Challenge   **What didn't go well today?**
_____
_____

Brain Dump
_____
_____
_____

Journal Prompt

Choose one of the prompts that resonates with you and write/draw/doodle what comes up for you.

Good Morning

Date: _____

Daily Intention — What do you want this day to be about?

_____
_____
_____

Today's Affirmation

_____
_____
_____

Actions	Self-Care
_____	_____
_____	_____
_____	_____
_____	_____

Good Evening

Today's Accomplishment — What went well today?

_____
_____

Today's Challenge — What didn't go well today?

_____
_____

Brain Dump

_____
_____
_____

Journal Prompt

Choose one of the prompts that resonates with you and write/draw/doodle what comes up for you.

Good Morning 🦋

Date: _____

Daily Intention — What do you want this day to be about?
_____
_____
_____

Today's Affirmation

Actions   Self-Care
_____   _____
_____   _____
_____   _____
_____   _____

Good Evening 🦋

Today's Accomplishment   What went well today?
_____
_____

Today's Challenge   What didn't go well today?
_____
_____

Brain Dump
_____
_____
_____

Journal Prompt

Choose one of the prompts that resonates with you and write/draw/doodle what comes up for you.

Good Morning

Date: _____

Daily Intention 　　　　　What do you want this day to be about?
_____
_____
_____

Today's Affirmation

Actions 　　　　　　　　　Self-Care
_____   _____
_____   _____
_____   _____
_____   _____

Good Evening

Today's Accomplishment 　　　　　　　What went well today?
_____
_____

Today's Challenge 　　　　　　　　　What didn't go well today?
_____
_____

Brain Dump
_____
_____
_____

Journal Prompt

Choose one of the prompts that resonates with you and write/draw/doodle what comes up for you.

Good Morning

Date: _____

Daily Intention What do you want this day to be about?

_____
_____
_____

Today's Affirmation

_____
_____
_____

Actions **Self-Care**

_____ _____
_____ _____
_____ _____

Good Evening

Today's Accomplishment What went well today?

_____
_____

Today's Challenge What didn't go well today?

_____
_____

Brain Dump

_____
_____

Journal Prompt

Choose one of the prompts that resonates with you and write/draw/doodle what comes up for you.

Good Morning

Date: _____

Daily Intention — What do you want this day to be about?

_____
_____
_____

Today's Affirmation

Actions   **Self-Care**

_____   _____
_____   _____
_____   _____
_____   _____

Good Evening

Today's Accomplishment   What went well today?
_____
_____

Today's Challenge   What didn't go well today?
_____
_____

Brain Dump
_____
_____
_____

Journal Prompt

Choose one of the prompts that resonates with you and write/draw/doodle what comes up for you.

Weekly Reflection

What went well this week?

_____

What changes have you noticed when it comes to your self-esteem and self-confidence?

_____

What resistance, if any, have you felt to this process? How might you shift this?

_____

Self-Esteem Scale

Self-Esteem /confidence action for the coming week?

Good Morning

Date: _____

Daily Intention
What do you want this day to be about?

_____
_____
_____

Today's Affirmation

_____

Actions
_____
_____
_____
_____

Self-Care
_____
_____
_____

Good Evening

Today's Accomplishment
What went well today?
_____
_____

Today's Challenge
What didn't go well today?
_____
_____

Brain Dump
_____
_____
_____

Journal Prompt

Choose one of the prompts that resonates with you and write/draw/doodle what comes up for you.

Good Morning

Date: _____

Daily Intention — What do you want this day to be about?
_____
_____
_____

Today's Affirmation

Actions   **Self-Care**
_____   _____
_____   _____
_____   _____

Good Evening

Today's Accomplishment   **What went well today?**
_____

Today's Challenge   **What didn't go well today?**
_____

Brain Dump
_____
_____

Journal Prompt

Choose one of the prompts that resonates with you and write/draw/doodle what comes up for you.

Good Morning

Date: _____

Daily Intention — What do you want this day to be about?

_____
_____
_____

Today's Affirmation

Actions	Self-Care
_____	_____
_____	_____
_____	_____
_____	_____

Good Evening

Today's Accomplishment — What went well today?
_____
_____

Today's Challenge — What didn't go well today?
_____
_____

Brain Dump
_____
_____
_____

Journal Prompt

Choose one of the prompts that resonates with you and write/draw/doodle what comes up for you.

Good Morning

Date: _____

Daily Intention

What do you want this day to be about?

_____
_____
_____

Today's Affirmation

Actions	Self-Care
_____	_____
_____	_____
_____	_____
_____	_____

Good Evening

Today's Accomplishment   What went well today?

_____
_____

Today's Challenge   What didn't go well today?

_____
_____

Brain Dump

_____
_____
_____

Journal Prompt

Choose one of the prompts that resonates with you and write/draw/doodle what comes up for you.

Good Morning

Date: _____

Daily Intention — What do you want this day to be about?

_____
_____
_____

Today's Affirmation

Actions	Self-Care
_____	_____
_____	_____
_____	_____
_____	_____

Good Evening

Today's Accomplishment — What went well today?

_____
_____

Today's Challenge — What didn't go well today?

_____
_____

Brain Dump

_____
_____
_____

Journal Prompt

Choose one of the prompts that resonates with you and write/draw/doodle what comes up for you.

Good Morning

Date: _____

Daily Intention — What do you want this day to be about?

_____
_____
_____

Today's Affirmation

_____

Actions	Self-Care
_____	_____
_____	_____
_____	_____
_____	_____

Good Evening

Today's Accomplishment — What went well today?

_____
_____

Today's Challenge — What didn't go well today?

_____
_____

Brain Dump

_____
_____
_____

Journal Prompt

Choose one of the prompts that resonates with you and write/draw/doodle what comes up for you.

Good Morning 🦋

Date: _____

Daily Intention

What do you want this day to be about?

_____
_____
_____

Today's Affirmation

Actions

_____
_____
_____
_____

Self-Care

_____
_____
_____
_____

Good Evening 🦋

Today's Accomplishment

What went well today?

_____
_____

Today's Challenge

What didn't go well today?

_____
_____

Brain Dump

_____
_____
_____

Journal Prompt

Choose one of the prompts that resonates with you and write/draw/doodle what comes up for you.

Weekly Reflection

What went well this week?

_____
_____
_____
_____
_____
_____

What changes have you noticed when it comes to your self-esteem and self-confidence?

_____
_____
_____
_____
_____
_____

What resistance, if any, have you felt to this process? How might you shift this?

_____
_____
_____
_____
_____

Self-Esteem Scale	Self-Esteem /confidence action for the coming week?

Good Morning

Date: _____

Daily Intention — What do you want this day to be about?

_____
_____
_____

Today's Affirmation

_____
_____
_____

Actions	Self-Care
_____	_____
_____	_____
_____	_____

Good Evening

Today's Accomplishment — What went well today?

_____
_____

Today's Challenge — What didn't go well today?

_____
_____

Brain Dump

_____
_____
_____

Journal Prompt

Choose one of the prompts that resonates with you and write/draw/doodle what comes up for you.

Good Morning

Date: _____

Daily Intention — What do you want this day to be about?

_____
_____
_____

Today's Affirmation

_____
_____
_____

Actions	Self-Care
_____	_____
_____	_____
_____	_____
_____	_____

Good Evening

Today's Accomplishment — What went well today?

_____
_____

Today's Challenge — What didn't go well today?

_____
_____

Brain Dump

_____
_____
_____

Journal Prompt

Choose one of the prompts that resonates with you and write/draw/doodle what comes up for you.

Good Morning

Date: _____

Daily Intention   What do you want this day to be about?

_____
_____
_____

Today's Affirmation

_____

Actions   Self-Care

_____   _____
_____   _____
_____   _____
_____   _____

Good Evening

Today's Accomplishment   What went well today?

_____
_____

Today's Challenge   What didn't go well today?

_____
_____

Brain Dump

_____
_____
_____

Journal Prompt

Choose one of the prompts that resonates with you and write/draw/doodle what comes up for you.

169

Good Morning 🦋

Date: _____

Daily Intention — What do you want this day to be about?
_____
_____
_____

Today's Affirmation

[highlighted box]

Actions   Self-Care
_____   _____
_____   _____
_____   _____
_____   _____

Good Evening 🦋

Today's Accomplishment   What went well today?
_____
_____

Today's Challenge   What didn't go well today?
_____
_____

Brain Dump
_____
_____
_____

Journal Prompt

Choose one of the prompts that resonates with you and write/draw/doodle what comes up for you.

Good Morning

Date: _____

Daily Intention What do you want this day to be about?

_____
_____
_____

Today's Affirmation

\

Actions   **Self-Care**

_____   _____
_____   _____
_____   _____
_____   _____

Good Evening

Today's Accomplishment   What went well today?

_____
_____

Today's Challenge   What didn't go well today?

_____
_____

Brain Dump

_____
_____
_____

Journal Prompt

Choose one of the prompts that resonates with you and write/draw/doodle what comes up for you.

Good Morning

Date: _____

Daily Intention ⸺ What do you want this day to be about?

_____
_____
_____

Today's Affirmation

Actions ⸺ **Self-Care**

_____ _____
_____ _____
_____ _____
_____ _____

Good Evening

Today's Accomplishment ⸺ What went well today?

_____
_____

Today's Challenge ⸺ What didn't go well today?

_____
_____

Brain Dump

_____
_____
_____

Journal Prompt

Choose one of the prompts that resonates with you and write/draw/doodle what comes up for you.

175

Good Morning 🦋

Date: _____

Daily Intention — What do you want this day to be about?

_____
_____
_____

Today's Affirmation

_____
_____
_____

Actions	Self-Care
_____	_____
_____	_____
_____	_____
_____	_____

Good Evening 🦋

Today's Accomplishment — What went well today?
_____
_____

Today's Challenge — What didn't go well today?
_____
_____

Brain Dump
_____
_____
_____

Journal Prompt

Choose one of the prompts that resonates with you and write/draw/doodle what comes up for you.

Weekly Reflection

What went well this week?

_____
_____
_____
_____
_____
_____
_____

What changes have you noticed when it comes to your self-esteem and self-confidence?

_____
_____
_____
_____
_____
_____
_____

What resistance, if any, have you felt to this process? How might you shift this?

_____
_____
_____
_____
_____
_____

Self-Esteem Scale

Self-Esteem /confidence action for the coming week?

Date: _____

Good Morning

Daily Intention   What do you want this day to be about?

_____
_____
_____

Today's Affirmation

_____

Actions	**Self-Care**
_____	_____
_____	_____
_____	_____
_____	_____

Good Evening

Today's Accomplishment   What went well today?

_____
_____

Today's Challenge   What didn't go well today?

_____
_____

Brain Dump

_____
_____
_____

Journal Prompt

Choose one of the prompts that resonates with you and write/draw/doodle what comes up for you.

180

Good Morning

Date: _____

Daily Intention — What do you want this day to be about?
_____
_____
_____

Today's Affirmation

```
[                                           ]
```

Actions   **Self-Care**
_____   _____
_____   _____
_____   _____

Good Evening

Today's Accomplishment   **What went well today?**
_____
_____

Today's Challenge   **What didn't go well today?**
_____
_____

Brain Dump
_____
_____
_____

Journal Prompt

Choose one of the prompts that resonates with you and write/draw/doodle what comes up for you.

Good Morning

Date: _____

Daily Intention — What do you want this day to be about?

_____
_____
_____

Today's Affirmation

_____

Actions	Self-Care
_____	_____
_____	_____
_____	_____
_____	_____

Good Evening

Today's Accomplishment — What went well today?

_____
_____

Today's Challenge — What didn't go well today?

_____
_____

Brain Dump

_____
_____
_____

Journal Prompt

Choose one of the prompts that resonates with you and write/draw/doodle what comes up for you.

Good Morning

Date: _____

Daily Intention   What do you want this day to be about?

_____
_____
_____

Today's Affirmation

Actions   Self-Care

_____   _____
_____   _____
_____   _____
_____   _____

Good Evening

Today's Accomplishment   What went well today?

_____
_____

Today's Challenge   What didn't go well today?

_____
_____

Brain Dump

_____
_____
_____

Journal Prompt

Choose one of the prompts that resonates with you and write/draw/doodle what comes up for you.

Good Morning

Date: _____

Daily Intention What do you want this day to be about?

_____
_____
_____

Today's Affirmation

_____

Actions   **Self-Care**

_____   _____
_____   _____
_____   _____

Good Evening

Today's Accomplishment   What went well today?

_____
_____

Today's Challenge   What didn't go well today?

_____
_____

Brain Dump

_____
_____
_____

Journal Prompt

Choose one of the prompts that resonates with you and write/draw/doodle what comes up for you.

Good Morning

Date: _____

Daily Intention — What do you want this day to be about?

_____
_____
_____

Today's Affirmation

_____

Actions	Self-Care
_____	_____
_____	_____
_____	_____
_____	_____

Good Evening

Today's Accomplishment — What went well today?

_____
_____

Today's Challenge — What didn't go well today?

_____
_____

Brain Dump

_____
_____

Journal Prompt

Choose one of the prompts that resonates with you and write/draw/doodle what comes up for you.

Good Morning

Date: _____

Daily Intention — What do you want this day to be about?

_____
_____
_____

Today's Affirmation

Actions   Self-Care

_____   _____
_____   _____
_____   _____
_____   _____

Good Evening

Today's Accomplishment   What went well today?
_____
_____

Today's Challenge   What didn't go well today?
_____
_____

Brain Dump
_____
_____
_____

Journal Prompt

Choose one of the prompts that resonates with you and write/draw/doodle what comes up for you.

Weekly Reflection

What went well this week?

_____
_____
_____
_____
_____
_____
_____

What changes have you noticed when it comes to your self-esteem and self-confidence?

_____
_____
_____
_____
_____
_____
_____

What resistance, if any, have you felt to this process? How might you shift this?

_____
_____
_____
_____
_____
_____

Self-Esteem Scale

Self-Esteem /confidence action for the coming week?

Good Morning

Date: _____

Daily Intention — What do you want this day to be about?

_____
_____
_____

Today's Affirmation

Actions   **Self-Care**

_____   _____
_____   _____
_____   _____
_____   _____

Good Evening

Today's Accomplishment   **What went well today?**
_____
_____

Today's Challenge   **What didn't go well today?**
_____
_____

Brain Dump
_____
_____
_____

Journal Prompt

Choose one of the prompts that resonates with you and write/draw/doodle what comes up for you.

Good Morning

Date: _____

Daily Intention — What do you want this day to be about?

_____
_____
_____

Today's Affirmation

_____
_____
_____

Actions	Self-Care
_____	_____
_____	_____
_____	_____
_____	_____

Good Evening

Today's Accomplishment — What went well today?

_____
_____

Today's Challenge — What didn't go well today?

_____
_____

Brain Dump

_____
_____
_____

Journal Prompt

Choose one of the prompts that resonates with you and write/draw/doodle what comes up for you.

Good Morning

Date: _____

Daily Intention — What do you want this day to be about?

_____
_____
_____

Today's Affirmation

_____

Actions

_____
_____
_____
_____

Self-Care

_____
_____
_____

Good Evening

Today's Accomplishment — What went well today?

_____
_____

Today's Challenge — What didn't go well today?

_____
_____

Brain Dump

_____
_____
_____

Journal Prompt

Choose one of the prompts that resonates with you and write/draw/doodle what comes up for you.

Good Morning

Date: _____

Daily Intention — What do you want this day to be about?

_____
_____
_____

Today's Affirmation

_____

Actions	Self-Care
_____	_____
_____	_____
_____	_____

Good Evening

Today's Accomplishment — What went well today?

_____
_____

Today's Challenge — What didn't go well today?

_____
_____

Brain Dump

_____
_____
_____

Journal Prompt

Choose one of the prompts that resonates with you and write/draw/doodle what comes up for you.

Good Morning

Date: _____

Daily Intention — What do you want this day to be about?

_____
_____
_____

Today's Affirmation

Actions	Self-Care
_____	_____
_____	_____
_____	_____
_____	_____

Good Evening

Today's Accomplishment — What went well today?
_____
_____

Today's Challenge — What didn't go well today?
_____
_____

Brain Dump
_____
_____
_____

Journal Prompt

Choose one of the prompts that resonates with you and write/draw/doodle what comes up for you.

Good Morning 🦋

Date: _____

Daily Intention   What do you want this day to be about?

_____
_____
_____

Today's Affirmation

_____
_____
_____

Actions   **Self-Care**

_____   _____
_____   _____
_____   _____
_____   _____

Good Evening 🦋

Today's Accomplishment   What went well today?

_____
_____

Today's Challenge   What didn't go well today?

_____
_____

Brain Dump

_____
_____
_____

Journal Prompt

Choose one of the prompts that resonates with you and write/draw/doodle what comes up for you.

Good Morning

Date: _____

Daily Intention — What do you want this day to be about?

_____
_____
_____

Today's Affirmation

Actions	Self-Care
_____	_____
_____	_____
_____	_____
_____	_____

Good Evening

Today's Accomplishment — What went well today?

_____
_____

Today's Challenge — What didn't go well today?

_____
_____

Brain Dump

_____
_____
_____

Journal Prompt

Choose one of the prompts that resonates with you and write/draw/doodle what comes up for you.

Weekly Reflection

What went well this week?

_____
_____
_____
_____
_____
_____
_____

What changes have you noticed when it comes to your self-esteem and self-confidence?

_____
_____
_____
_____
_____
_____
_____
_____

What resistance, if any, have you felt to this process? How might you shift this?

_____
_____
_____
_____
_____
_____
_____

Self-Esteem Scale

Self-Esteem /confidence action for the coming week?

Good Morning

Date: _____

Daily Intention — What do you want this day to be about?

_____
_____
_____

Today's Affirmation

_____
_____
_____

Actions	Self-Care
_____	_____
_____	_____
_____	_____
_____	_____

Good Evening

Today's Accomplishment — What went well today?

_____
_____

Today's Challenge — What didn't go well today?

_____
_____

Brain Dump

_____
_____
_____

Journal Prompt

Choose one of the prompts that resonates with you and write/draw/doodle what comes up for you.

Good Morning

Date: _____

Daily Intention — What do you want this day to be about?
_____
_____
_____

Today's Affirmation

Actions	Self-Care
_____	_____
_____	_____
_____	_____
_____	_____

Good Evening

Today's Accomplishment — What went well today?
_____
_____

Today's Challenge — What didn't go well today?
_____
_____

Brain Dump
_____
_____
_____

Journal Prompt

Choose one of the prompts that resonates with you and write/draw/doodle what comes up for you.

Good Morning

Date: _____

Daily Intention — What do you want this day to be about?

_____
_____
_____

Today's Affirmation

Actions   **Self-Care**

_____   _____
_____   _____
_____   _____

Good Evening

Today's Accomplishment   **What went well today?**

_____
_____

Today's Challenge   **What didn't go well today?**

_____
_____

Brain Dump

_____
_____

Journal Prompt

Choose one of the prompts that resonates with you and write/draw/doodle what comes up for you.

214

Good Morning

Date: _____

Daily Intention   What do you want this day to be about?

_____
_____
_____

Today's Affirmation

_____
_____
_____

Actions   **Self-Care**

_____   _____
_____   _____
_____   _____
_____   _____

Good Evening

Today's Accomplishment   What went well today?
_____
_____

Today's Challenge   What didn't go well today?
_____
_____

Brain Dump
_____
_____
_____

Journal Prompt

Choose one of the prompts that resonates with you and write/draw/doodle what comes up for you.

Good Morning

Date: _____

Daily Intention — What do you want this day to be about?

_____
_____
_____

Today's Affirmation

_____

Actions

_____
_____
_____
_____

Self-Care

_____
_____
_____
_____

Good Evening

Today's Accomplishment — What went well today?

_____
_____

Today's Challenge — What didn't go well today?

_____
_____

Brain Dump

_____
_____
_____

Journal Prompt

Choose one of the prompts that resonates with you and write/draw/doodle what comes up for you.

Good Morning

Date: _____

Daily Intention   What do you want this day to be about?

_____
_____
_____

Today's Affirmation

_____

Actions	Self-Care
_____	_____
_____	_____
_____	_____
_____	_____

Good Evening

Today's Accomplishment   What went well today?

_____
_____

Today's Challenge   What didn't go well today?

_____
_____

Brain Dump

_____
_____
_____

Journal Prompt

Choose one of the prompts that resonates with you and write/draw/doodle what comes up for you.

Good Morning

Date: _____

Daily Intention   What do you want this day to be about?

_____
_____
_____

Today's Affirmation

_____

Actions	Self-Care
_____	_____
_____	_____
_____	_____
_____	_____

Good Evening

Today's Accomplishment   What went well today?
_____
_____

Today's Challenge   What didn't go well today?
_____
_____

Brain Dump
_____
_____
_____

Journal Prompt

Choose one of the prompts that resonates with you and write/draw/doodle what comes up for you.

Weekly Reflection

What went well this week?

_____
_____
_____
_____
_____
_____
_____

What changes have you noticed when it comes to your self-esteem and self- confidence?

_____
_____
_____
_____
_____
_____
_____

What resistance, if any, have you felt to this process? How might you shift this?

_____
_____
_____
_____
_____

Self-Esteem Scale

Self-Esteem /confidence action for the coming week?

Good Morning

Date: _____

Daily Intention   What do you want this day to be about?

_____
_____
_____

Today's Affirmation

Actions   **Self-Care**

_____   _____
_____   _____
_____   _____
_____

Good Evening

Today's Accomplishment   What went well today?
_____
_____

Today's Challenge   What didn't go well today?
_____
_____

Brain Dump
_____
_____
_____

Journal Prompt

Choose one of the prompts that resonates with you and write/draw/doodle what comes up for you.

Good Morning

Date: _____

Daily Intention — What do you want this day to be about?

_____
_____
_____

Today's Affirmation

Actions	Self-Care
_____	_____
_____	_____
_____	_____
_____	_____

Good Evening

Today's Accomplishment — What went well today?

_____
_____

Today's Challenge — What didn't go well today?

_____
_____

Brain Dump

_____
_____
_____

Journal Prompt

Choose one of the prompts that resonates with you and write/draw/doodle what comes up for you.

Good Morning

Date: _____

Daily Intention **What do you want this day to be about?**
_____
_____
_____

Today's Affirmation

Actions **Self-Care**
_____ _____
_____ _____
_____ _____
_____ _____

Good Evening

Today's Accomplishment **What went well today?**
_____
_____

Today's Challenge **What didn't go well today?**
_____
_____

Brain Dump
_____
_____
_____

Journal Prompt

Choose one of the prompts that resonates with you and write/draw/doodle what comes up for you.

25 affirmations to help boost self-esteem and self-confidence

1. I am worthy of love and respect.
2. I believe in my abilities and express my true self with confidence.
3. I am proud of who I am and all that I have accomplished.
4. I trust myself to make the right decisions.
5. I embrace my unique qualities and celebrate my individuality.
6. I deserve success, happiness, and fulfillment.
7. I am capable of achieving my goals and dreams.
8. I release negative self-talk and embrace positive thoughts.
9. I am confident in my talents and skills.
10. I am enough, just as I am.
11. I am growing and improving every day.
12. I love and accept myself unconditionally.
13. I radiate self-confidence and inner strength.
14. I handle challenges with grace and resilience.
15. I attract positive energy and people into my life.
16. I am deserving of all the good things that come my way.
17. I am strong, capable, and courageous.
18. I value my own opinions and trust my intuition.
19. I speak my truth with confidence and clarity.
20. I am in control of my own happiness.
21. I honor my commitments to myself and others.
22. I am worthy of success in every area of my life.
23. I am open to new opportunities and embrace change with confidence.
24. I forgive myself for past mistakes and learn from them.
25. I am a powerful creator of my own life.

Notes